SECRET
SUNDERLAND

Marie Gardiner

AMBERLEY

About the Author

Marie Gardiner is a writer and photographer from Sunderland who now lives in County Durham. After graduating with a degree in film and media, Marie embarked on a career in broadcasting, with a particular interest in history and documentary production. Her recent work includes educational articles around film and photography, *Sunderland, Industrial Giant* – a book chronicling twentieth-century working life in Sunderland – and a number of film documentaries about how communities responded to the First World War.

First published 2019

Amberley Publishing
The Hill, Stroud
Gloucestershire, GL5 4EP

www.amberley-books.com

ISBN 978 1 4456 8409 3 (print)
ISBN 978 1 4456 8410 9 (ebook)

British Library Cataloguing in Publication Data.
A catalogue record for this book is available from the British Library.

Origination by Amberley Publishing.
Printed in Great Britain.

Contents

Introduction

And above all, watch with glittering eyes the whole world around you because the greatest secrets are always hidden in the most unlikely places.

Roald Dahl

Growing out of the original townships of Bishopwearmouth on the south side of the river, Monkwearmouth on the north and Sunderland (sundered land), the city of Sunderland now boasts a population of almost 300,000 people. Deeply connected to its prosperous industrial past, Sunderland does enjoy a good hark back, and given half a chance, any Mackem (a Sunderland native) will be glad to tell you what used to be where, and why you should pay particular attention to a building.

Secret is a relatively flexible term here. We can sometimes make the mistake of assuming that because we're entrenched in or passionate about something, that everyone else must be aware of it, too. I've tried to take off my 'history-loving-Mackem' hat and look

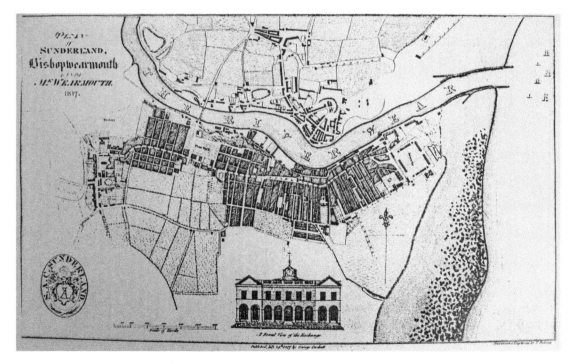

Bishopwearmouth, Monkwearmouth and Sunderland – the original townships. (Sunderland Museum and Winter Gardens)

with fresh eyes at my home city. In doing this, I've added knowledge to stories I already knew, I've delighted in brand-new aspects I'd not heard of before and I've been able to share some of the really fascinating parts of Sunderland's rich history.

So, take a trip with me to discover how a terrible tragedy, resulting in the death of almost 200, changed UK law. Walk through the East End to uncover mass graves, bodysnatching and an old maritime hero. Find out why we have a concrete boat stuck on the bed of the River Wear, how our beloved football club was formed by a Scotsman, and how Sunderland is connected to one of Victorian England's most notorious murderers.

If you're from the area, I hope you'll find things that let you turn to your friend smugly and say, 'I knew that.' I hope, too, you'll find a few things you didn't know, things that might shock, delight and appal you in equal measure. And if you're not a Mackem, I hope you enjoy this little literary tour of our city by the sea, and see that Sunderland is a place bursting with history, with culture and with heart.

DID YOU KNOW?
The rivalry between Sunderland and Newcastle has been around long before the days of football. Charles I favoured Newcastle over Sunderland in the coal trade, to Sunderland's detriment, and so during the Civil War in 1642, Newcastle backed the king and Sunderland supported the Parliamentarians. The fight culminated in the Battle of Boldon Hill where Sunderland (backed by the Scots) won and as a result the Parliamentarians backed Sunderland over Newcastle during the Commonwealth.

1. Heroes, Villains and People of Note

Harry Watts – Lifesaver

Harry (or Henry) Watts, born in 1826, was a sailor and diver from Sunderland's East End who grew up in relative poverty. The youngest of five children, Harry had a difficult childhood: his mother died when he was just seven, and his father spent much of his time bed-bound. At just nine years old Harry became the family's main earner, taking a job first at Garrison Pottery and later at a weaving factory. Eventually, though, he turned to the sea.

At fourteen, Harry signed up as an apprentice sailor and was shipped off to Quebec. It was there that he made his first rescue when one of his friends, a lad named Nicholson, fell overboard.

After Quebec, while in London, Harry found out his father had died and his two sisters and brother were now homeless, so he had his captain, Captain Luckley, send them some savings.

His second rescue came in Miramichi (also in Canada) where he saved the life of Luckley after his canoe capsized. Jumping into the water, he fastened a rope around him and helped him to the ship's ladder.

Harry Watts in his diving outfit. (Sunderland Museum and Winter Gardens)

So it continued, and by the age of nineteen Watts had already saved five lives. In 1846, at twenty years of age, he married Rebecca Smith. Both orphans and both without a home, they set up house in Silver Street in Sunderland and tried to make the best of what little they had.

The following year Harry returned to the sea in a vessel called the *Express*, travelling to Rotterdam. While watching six seamen working on their ship from a boat, he witnessed the anchor rope directly above them break. The anchor crashed into the boat 'smashing it like an eggshell and throwing the men in all directions'. Harry leapt into the chaos and reached the men in time to save them all.

Having had enough of life on the sea for a while, he returned to Sunderland and worked as a rigger in the shipyards until 1853. While he was there, he pulled another five people out of the River Wear, bringing his lifesaving total up to fourteen. His fifteenth was the sad case of a young woman who attempted to take her own life by drowning herself in the sea. Harry saved her, but the next day she was charged with attempting to commit suicide and he was forced to give evidence. Thankfully good sense prevailed and the woman was discharged.

Harry couldn't resist the call of the sea, but it wasn't long before tragedy was to strike. He was returning home to Sunderland from London when gales struck and shifted the ship's cargo, forcing it to run ashore just off the South Pier. A lifeboat was launched and the crew rescued, but on seeing her husband coming ashore in the lifeboat, Harry's wife Rebecca waded out to meet him. The exposure to the wet and cold caused her to fall ill and later die.

Harry Watts with his medals, 1910.
(Sunderland Museum and Winter Gardens)

Watts was employed by the River Wear Commissioners in 1861, and was also a member of the Sunderland Lifeboat and Life Brigade services. He remarried and had two children, joined the Primitive Methodist Church and gave up alcohol entirely. His lifesaving total was now up to seventeen, but still hadn't been recognised in any official capacity:

> Such neglect, such indifference to heroic services in the cause of humanity is probably without a parallel. To a man actuated by any other than the highest motive, this lack of appreciation would surely have acted as a deterrent in this humane work, but greatly to Mr Watts' credit he continued that work, and again and again, and yet again, risked his own life to save others. (Extract *from Life of Harry Watts; Sixty Years Sailor & Diver* by Alfred Spencer)

Watts' brave deeds were eventually rewarded in the form of a medal presentation in the late 1860s. These were unfortunately stolen from an exhibition a decade later, and the story goes the thief's daughter threw them into the fire after tiring of playing with them. The people of Sunderland weren't ready to let Harry's deeds be forgotten though, and the townspeople grouped together to buy him new medals, which were eventually gifted to Sunderland Museum, where they remain to this day. Harry Watts died in April 1913 at the age of eighty-six but left behind a legacy of divers, with both his son and his grandson following in his footsteps.

DID YOU KNOW?
Sunderland helped to launch Stan Laurel (of Laurel and Hardy) after he landed his first proper role in *Sleeping Beauty* (with his Wearside-based pal Benny Barron) when it started its national tour at the King's Theatre on Crowtree Road. He appeared under his real name, Stanley Jefferson.

Stormy Petrel – (another) Lifesaver

Son of a joiner, Joseph Ray Hodgson was born in Dunning Street, Bishopwearmouth, in 1829, meaning he was just three years younger than Sunderland's other renowned saver of lives, Harry Watts. He made his first recorded rescue as a young teen, pulling three-year-old John Snowdon from the river. Rescuing wood carver John Marshall from the Wear a few years later earned him a trade when Marshall decided to repay him by training him as a carver and gilder.

Through the years, Hodgson rescued many more souls, both individuals he pulled out of the river and as part of a rescue team coming to the aid of boats and ships. He could often be seen on the pier searching for ships in distress, particularly when there was a storm brewing on the North Sea. This earned him the nickname 'Stormy Petrel' after the sea bird thought to be the last to come ashore in a storm. It's believed that hundreds of people owe their lives to him.

Stormy Petrel's blue plaque on The Boar's Head pub.

Keel Square, where Stormy Petrel's blue plaque will be relocated.

Hodgson was awarded a gold medal from Napoleon III for the rescue of French schooner *Les Trois Soeurs*, and a silver medal from the Board of Trade for Gallantry in Saving Life at Sea. Later, he was honoured for the rescue of a man from the Regent's Canal Docks (London) by the Royal Humane Society, but as no records exist to support that it's more likely that it was from Sunderland Humane Society.

Despite Hodgson moving from Sunderland to London, the Mayor of Sunderland awarded him another gold medal in 1883, this one reading, 'As a token of respect and esteem by a few Sunderland friends, to whom his many perilous exploits and daring achievements are well known.'

A markedly sadder end than his contemporary Harry Watts, Joseph Hodgson died a pauper, having been forced to sell his medals to pay for a room in a slum area of London. He is buried in Newham where his epitaph reads: 'A Brave And Unselfish Man Risking His Own Life To Save Others From Shipwrecks.'

Although Hodgson's actions affected so many lives, his heroic deeds soon faded with the passage of time. Many years later, his great-great-granddaughters were researching their family tree and came across his story. Not wanting his actions to slip out of consciousness altogether, they started a campaign for Hodgson to have his own blue plaque in Sunderland, commemorating his life-saving actions. They were successful, and in June 2018 a plaque was unveiled on The Boar's Head, a bistro near to the Port of Sunderland. The event was attended by relatives of Hodgson and the Mayor of Sunderland. The plaque will remain for two years and then will be moved to a permanent site on Keel Square so that the city will have a prominent and lasting reminder of the man who saved so many lives.

Mary Ann Cotton – the Victorian Murderess

Born on 31 October 1832 in Low Moorsley, Mary Ann Cotton (née Robson) had a mostly uneventful childhood. After her father, a pitman, died in a fall when she was a young teen, Cotton became a nurse to help support her family. At twenty, she left home and married William Mowbray, moving to Devon for five years, during which time they had five children. On coming back to County Durham, four of those children had died as a result of gastric fever. The family moved around, before eventually settling in Sunderland, during which time Mary had given birth to three more children. They died – as did William – of an intestinal problem in 1865. His life was insured and so Mary Ann was able to collect a payout of £35.

Working in Sunderland Infirmary, Cotton met an engineer called George Ward. George was to be her next husband, but not for long; he died fourteen months after they were married, leaving her another substantial insurance payment. A month later, Cotton got a job as a housekeeper for a widower with a young family called James Robinson. A week after Cotton started work, Robinson's ten-month-old son died from what was officially documented as gastric fever. The start of 1867 was tragic: Cotton's last child by her first husband died, as did two more of Robinson's children and Mary's mother. Despite what seemed like a run of terrible luck, Robinson and Cotton married and had two more children. Theirs was not a happy union, with the couple quickly in debt and constantly fighting. History was to repeat itself once again and one of the children died before their first birthday. Cotton left Robinson (or perhaps was forced to leave) after he refused to

The teapot used to brew the tea with which Mary Ann Cotton poisoned her victims. (Beamish Living Museum of the North)

take out life insurance. It's possible he had become suspicious of the great number of deaths surrounding Mary Ann.

In 1870, Mary Ann met a chap called Frederick Cotton, whose wife and children had passed away before they met. His sister, Margaret, suspiciously died of stomach pains shortly after the meeting. Already pregnant with his child, Mary Ann married Frederick in late September of the same year. Legally she was still married to Robinson, having never divorced him and having left while he was still alive. Frederick became ill with stomach pains and died just over a year later.

Mary had insured both Frederick and his children. By the time Frederick was ill, Mary Ann had already moved on to the next man, Joseph Nattrass. Needing work, she took employment nursing a Mr Quick-Manning, who was suffering from smallpox. She became involved with Quick-Manning and within weeks, her son, stepson and Nattrass were all dead.

Mary once again got pregnant, but Quick-Manning wouldn't marry her, so she was forced to look for extra work. She explained to an overseer, Thomas Riley, that she needed to look after her stepson Charles and asked whether Charles could work in the workhouse without her needing to be there. When she was told he couldn't, an offhand comment about how she wouldn't be troubled with him much longer was the beginning of her downfall. Charles died a week later and Riley reported his suspicions to the police.

Cotton was almost saved by the initial inquest, which returned a verdict of natural causes, but the doctor had doubts and ran some tests on the stomach and internal organs of her victims. This revealed arsenic, which is tasteless and causes similar effects to other medical conditions common at the time, like dysentery and gastric fever: vomiting, diarrhoea and abdominal pains. Arsenic was cheap and easily available from the chemist to use as a pesticide for bedbugs.

Cotton was arrested and the police strove to find more evidence, exhuming some of the bodies of others who had died in her presence or care. In these remains they also found traces of arsenic. Mary Ann was accused of murdering her stepsons Charles and Robert, lodger and lover Joseph Nattrass, her mother, and her 'husband' Frederick Cotton. Due to

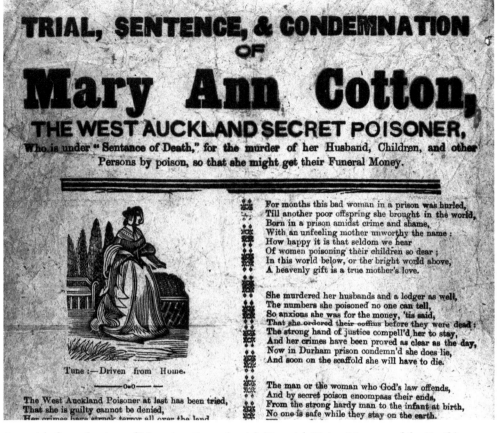

An article from the time of Mary Ann Cotton's trial. (Beamish Living Museum of the North)

poor record-keeping and less than ideal conditions generally at that time, she was only tried for the murder of Charles, and in March of 1873 was found guilty in less than ninety minutes and sentenced to be hanged. She'd given birth to another child in January while in custody, a girl.

Mary Ann Cotton's black Wedgewood teapot, in which she allegedly brewed the arsenic, and the stool from her prison cell are now in the care of Beamish Living Museum of the North, but how they came to be there is an interesting tale of mystery. The teapot arrived in 1972 without background or context. In 1989, the museum received a letter from the donor's daughter:

The local GP who donated it had inherited it, via his step-mother, from his step-grandmother – the wife of a GP in West Auckland, County Durham where Cotton was living in 1872 at the time of her arrest. His grandmother had been given the teapot by an old lady in West Auckland who had become very fond of her – a very strange gift as a token of affection! The donor had never felt comfortable with ownership of the macabre relic and was persuaded by his family to send it to Beamish, though he neglected to tell us of its origins at the time!' (Beamish Living Museum of the North)

The stool that Mary Ann Cotton had in her prison cell while incarcerated. (Beamish Living Museum of the North)

Although the authenticity of these items can't be verified beyond all doubt, it's highly likely that they are genuine. In a time when collecting macabre souvenirs was en vogue, gentlemen would often have a 'cabinet of curiosities', collections of all sorts designed to function as a social device, an early form of showing off to your mates.

It's not known exactly how many people Cotton killed, but estimates put it at as many as twenty-one, including eleven of her thirteen children. The two children who survived were George from her marriage to James Robinson, and the baby she had while in prison, Margaret Edith. The terrible actions of Mary Ann Cotton are one of the main reasons you can no longer insure the life of a child in the UK.

Jack Crawford – the Hero of Camperdown

If you walk through Mowbray Park, the pleasant Victorian park in the centre of Sunderland, you'll come across a statue of a man nailing a piece of cloth to a post. This is one of Sunderland's most proudly told stories, that of Jack Crawford – Hero of Camperdown.

In 1775 Jack was born in Pottery Bank in the east end of Sunderland. He apprenticed as a sailor around the age of twelve, serving on the *Peggy*, and in the mid-1790s he joined the Navy, where many speculate he was probably recruited by force – press ganged. Although there's no evidence to support this, it was common practice at the time, as life in the Navy was hard; there was very little in the way of pay, and both food and accommodation were poor, so it was difficult to get people to join.

During his time in the Royal Navy, Crawford served under Admiral Duncan on HMS *Venerable*. At this time, the French were conducting a successful land campaign as part of the French Revolutionary Wars. Having conquered Holland and joined forces with Spain, next on their list was Ireland to be used as a springboard for a possible invasion of England. English fleets were blockading enemy ports, and to the north, Admiral Duncan

A drawing of Jack Crawford nailing the flag to the mast. (Sunderland Museum and Winter Gardens)

was charged with watching the Dutch fleet. Having subdued Holland, the French declared it a republic, to be called the Batavian Republic. On the 11 October 1797, Duncan engaged with the Dutch Navy off the coast of a village called Camperduin (Camperdown) near Bergen. The fighting raged and the fleets were heavily engaged. During this, the mast of the *Venerable* was hit, breaking off the top part and causing the flag to fall to the ground.

While it might seem like a small thing, the lowering of an admiral's flag (or colours) during battle could be an indication to his fleet to surrender. This would be disastrous for the British, and the story goes that Admiral Duncan asked for a volunteer to replace the flag. I'm sure you've guessed by now that that volunteer was none other than Jack Crawford. Crawford climbed the remains of the mast and nailed the flag to it, taking a splinter to the cheek from shots fired while he was up there. The Dutch fleet were beaten in the Battle of Camperdown without a single British ship being lost.

After the battle, Jack suffered lockjaw due to the splinter damage to his cheek, and needed to be fed through a quill for a short time. For his bravery in battle, Jack was presented to George III and given a yearly pension of £30. His was the name on everyone's lips and he was revered, particularly in his home town of Sunderland, where they awarded him a silver medal, engraved with 'The town of Sunderland to Jack Crawford, for gallant services. The 11th October 1797'.

Once he'd left the Navy, it was a sad little decline for Jack Crawford. He liked a drink, so his pension was often frittered away on booze, leaving him destitute. He sold his medal to raise money and there are many tales of him dining out on his heroism for the promise of a drink, including one odd rumour of him shouting abuse at police while riding a pig down the high street!

JACK CRAWFORD

THE

HERO

OF

CAMPERDOWN.

THE SAILOR WHO SO HEROICALLY NAILED ADMIRAL DUNCAN'S
FLAG TO THE MAIN-TOP-GALLANT-MAST OF H.M.S. VENERABLE IN THE
GLORIOUS ACTION OFF CAMPERDOWN, ON OCTOBER 11TH 1797,
JACK CRAWFORD WAS BORN AT THE POTTERY BANK SUNDERLAND 1775,
AND DIED IN HIS NATIVE TOWN 1831, AGED 56 YEARS.
ERECTED BY PUBLIC SUBSCRIPTION.

The statue of Jack Crawford in Mowbray Park.

A Jack Crawford-inspired artwork in Mowbray Park with the statue in the background.

During the cholera epidemic that was sweeping the town, Jack died (he was, in fact, only the second recorded victim) in November of 1831, and received a pauper's funeral, buried in an unmarked mass grave. Jack's son bought the medal back from the pawnbroker and it was eventually acquired by a descendant of Admiral Duncan, before finally being presented to Sunderland Museum, who still have it today. In the late 1880s, the town successfully petitioned to get Jack a gravestone, which was unveiled to a large crowd, reportedly using the flag he had nailed to the mast. The people of Sunderland had raised more than they needed for a headstone, and so a little later in 1890, the Mowbray Park statue was built with the surplus.

The story of Jack Crawford has another interesting slant, one that isn't often talked about. As mentioned, it was tough work in the Navy in Jack's time, and they had a hard

Jack Crawford's headstone in the cemetery next to Holy Trinity Church.

time recruiting; hence press gangs were created to force people into joining up. Awarding a regular, working-class man with a medal and the attention, pomp and ceremony that comes with that would inevitably be seen as inspirational by other men like Jack, encouraging many of them to join up in the hope that they too might get a taste of 'glory' or shared success. Indeed, it was only an upsurge of civic pride and subsequent renewed interest in the country's naval past that led to the public appeal for Jack's headstone. The power of propaganda has often worked, and it's a contentious point.

Regardless of the reasons behind his awards, the actions of Jack Crawford were certainly heroic and most definitely helped towards the success of the British fleet at Camperdown. Jack's legacy is lasting, and as well as the statue and headstone, Jack had poems and songs written about him, has been the subject of stories and documentaries, has been featured on pottery, and is the origin of the well-known phrase 'nail your colours to the mast'.

William Mills – Inventor

As inventors go, William Mills isn't exactly on the tip of everyone's tongue. He lacks the glamour of any of the big names, and there's yet to be a film featuring him, but (Sir) William Mills, who was born in Southwick in 1856, has plenty of accomplishments to his name.

Once his private education was complete (and after a brief time as a butcher), Mills worked under George Clarke as an apprentice, with duties like laying cables and salvaging ships. At the end of this apprenticeship, he was a fully qualified marine engineer with a first-class certificate. It was his time spent at sea during this apprenticeship that propelled him towards his first invention. Mills had witnessed a great loss of life while at sea and this was, in part, due to the often unsafe engaging and disengaging methods used on lifeboats, and so he invented a quick-release hook. This was exhibited in Liverpool at the Shipowners' Exhibition in 1886 and he was given a gold medal from the Mercantile Marine Service's Association as well as winning gold at the exhibition. His design was approved for use by the Board of Trade and ended up being used worldwide, and indeed a variation of his invention is still used today.

Mills soon set up an aluminium foundry, which is said to have been the first in Britain: William Mills Ltd, at Bonners Field, Monkwearmouth, where he patented and produced golf clubs, some of the earliest aluminium type, one of which was called the Mills putter and was highly sought-after by keen golfers. The factory produced a variety of things, including castings for the car industry, and they even had a stand at the Automobile Show at Crystal Palace in 1903. As the 'car scene' was all about the Midlands at that time, Mills relocated to just outside of Birmingham. There, as well as producing parts for the motor industry, they also dabbled in cooking utensils and roller skates – it was varied!

This is all very nice but you're probably wondering why Sunderland should get so excited about a guy who made some golf clubs and a colander. Well, aside from his potentially lifesaving quick-release hook mentioned earlier, Mills' standout achievement came on the back of the First World War. His factories produced lightweight castings for aircraft, which was still a very new enterprise. He opened a munitions factory in 1915 and it was here that he produced the Mills Bomb. Grenades had been around for

A replica Mills Bomb or Grenade.

a long time, but they were rudimentary and dangerous to the thrower. A version of the grenade in common use was thrown by using an 18-inch stick, which had a nasty habit of catching on something when flung. Mills came up with his own version, one that would be locked with a pin and had a fuse so there was time (only four seconds) to take cover before it went off. There were several incarnations of these Mills Bombs as they refined and improved the technique. In 1917 a revised model was released (No. 36M) which was dipped in shellac to help prevent deterioration, and the fuse lengthened to seven seconds. As the detonators were shipped separately, it wasn't unknown for soldiers to open a box of Mills Bombs only to find they were missing their detonators. Over 75 million of these grenades were produced during the course of the war, although not all of them by Mills' factories. It was for these services that he was given a knighthood in 1922.

William Mills died in 1932 but his business continued to thrive. It was called into service again during the Second World War, when the government took it under control and used it to produce aircraft engine castings, including parts for the Merlin engine used in Spitfires. Eventually it fizzled out and ceased to exist but William

'How a bomber flings a Mills Grenade' by Douglas Macpherson. (Sunderland Museum and Winter Gardens)

Mills lives on in his inventions that undoubtedly saved many lives, and best of all is it all started in Sunderland.

DID YOU KNOW?
In 1842, thousands of people gathered to watch Michael Smith, an American sailor, jump off the Wearmouth Bridge. Amazingly, he survived, and collected money from the crowd who were appreciative of his daring feat. Unfortunately his elation didn't last long, as he was arrested for begging!

Michael Smith, who jumped off the Wearmouth Bridge in 1842. (Sunderland Local Studies Library)

Kate Adie – Trailblazing Journalist

Although born in Whitley Bay in 1945, Kate Adie was raised by her adoptive parents in Sunderland. After earning her degree, Kate started her career as a station assistant at BBC Radio Durham, moving to Radio Bristol later as a producer. It wasn't long before she would move to television to report for local stations in the south, before joining the national news in the late 1970s working initially as a court correspondent.

In late April 1980 on a Wednesday morning, a group of six armed men attacked the Iranian Embassy in London. Twenty-six hostages were taken and the drama continued to unfold over six days. Kate Adie was the first reporter on the scene and broadcast live as the SAS stormed the embassy, interrupting the World Snooker Championships and reporting unscripted from behind a car door to one of the largest news audiences ever. This was to be a defining moment in Kate's career; thereafter she was regularly sent to troubled spots to report on war and conflict. In 1986 she was at the scene of the American bombing of Tripoli, and the Lockerbie bombing two years later. In 1989, she was given the position of chief news correspondent – a role she would occupy for the next fourteen years.

Kate Adie.
(Ken Lennox)

One of her first postings was to Tiananmen Square in China, where student-led protests for democracy were taking place. There was a violent response to the protests from the military and the number of deaths has been placed at over 10,000, many more than was reported at the time.

In 2003 Kate stepped back from reporting on the front line and instead took work as a freelance journalist and public speaker. She has honorary degrees from a number of universities and has won several awards both nationally and internationally for her work in journalism.

If you were to pay a visit to the University of Sunderland, where Kate is an Honorary Professor of Journalism, you can search through the Kate Adie Collection, an archive of material spanning her journalistic career, including reports, personal notebooks, tapes and videos.

In 2018 Kate was made a CBE for services to media in the Queen's Honours List and awarded the Bafta Fellowship for her contribution to television and the arts where she was described as, 'a truly ground-breaking news journalist, being one of a very small number of women working to report the news from hostile environments around the world.' While that trend is surely changing as more women claim their place in serious journalism, undoubtably it is Kate Adie who blazed that trail and inspired so many to follow in her footsteps.

2. Entertainment and Sport

The Sunderland Empire – the Jewel in Sunderland's Crown

One of Sunderland's instantly recognisable landmarks, the Sunderland Empire has had rather a rollercoaster of a history, with Sunderland at times collectively holding its breath to see if it will appear out of the other end of a bleak tunnel, or if they'll be left without their beloved theatre. If you're a native Mackem, or even just live in the North East, chances are you'll have been to a show at the Empire at some point, be that one of the grand West End musicals it now frequently hosts, or even just the traditional panto we've come to expect every Christmas. Things, however, were not always so prosperous.

The Empire opened in 1907, but only just. Three days before it was due to have its opening night, there was a fire on the roof, starting in a barrel of tar. Workmen pushed it over the side and it plummeted to the street, splashing, but thankfully missing, a man walking by.

The Sunderland Empire around 1907. (Sunderland Museum and Winter Gardens)

High Street West in the 1930s with the Empire visible in the background. (Sunderland Museum and Winter Gardens)

Built at a cost of £31,000, it was not only the biggest theatre in town it was also intended to be the safest, notwithstanding the hazard of flying, flaming tar'. (Alistair Robinson, *Sunderland Empire: A Centenary History*)

It was a sight to behold, with its 90-foot tower topped with the now iconic statue of Terpsichore, the Greek muse of dance, who stood on a then revolving globe with its lit Empire sign. The capacity of the theatre was 3,000 and there was rapturous applause when, prior to the show, the house lights were put up so that everyone could appreciate the theatre's stunning decor. Vesta Tilley (real name Matilda Alice Powles), who'd shot to fame as a music hall performer with her male impersonator act, was the guest of honour at the opening. A star from the young age of eleven, at the time of the Empire's opening she'd been performing for thirty-eight years.

Over the years, the stage would be graced with stars of all kinds, and not always human. Hans the musical pony was a firm favourite, as were the cricketing elephants and a 'highly intelligent' horse called Mascot.

When the Second World War started in 1939, the Sunderland Empire was closed, as were any large places where crowds might gather and become vulnerable in an attack. There were protests, and among the voices the most notable was perhaps George Bernard Shaw who reminded everyone that theatres and entertainment were pretty integral for soldiers on leave, not to mention for morale generally. He had a point, so the theatre reopened on the proviso it would close at 10 p.m. each evening.

Terpsichore (the fibreglass replacement), 2018.

The Empire ticked along for a while and it got through the war mostly unscathed (Terpsichore was removed after being damaged by a nearby bomb blast), but its momentum was starting to dwindle. In 1947, it had reached the grand age of forty, but things weren't going so well.

> An article in the *Sunderland Echo* of 30 June that year praised the theatre's managers for booking nothing but the 'best available,' but castigated audiences for giving the place a bad reputation. Support from the public was often "sadly lacking," said the writer.' (Alistair Robinson, *Sunderland Empire a Centenary History*)

In 1954, Ken Dodd played his second professional date at the Empire having only had his debut a few days prior, returning again the next May. Dodd would become a regular in Sunderland, saying he had a soft spot for the area and that he felt appreciated there. The local critics weren't so fond of him at first, describing him as 'a comedian of dreadful demeanour'. In 1959 the theatre couldn't sustain itself any longer and finally ground to a halt, closing as a privately run venue.

Sunderland Corporation, the local authority of the time, had been looking for a new civic hall. The Victoria Hall had been destroyed by bombing for which the government had provided compensation, and it was with this money that they were able to purchase the Empire.

The Sunderland Empire dress circle.

By 1972 the Empire was looking a little tired and tatty and so it was given a makeover. They replaced many of the seats, created new entrances, redecorated and added floodlights to the outside. The original Terpsichore – made of bronze – had sat gathering dust in storage since its removal in the Second World War, was taken out and put on display inside the theatre. In its original position atop the globe was a fibreglass replacement.

You may remember I mentioned about Sunderland's reputation for being a decidedly hard audience to impress. Comedians, in particular, often got a rough ride, and it was frequently referred to as 'the comic's graveyard'. This led to a particularly ironic twist of fate in 1976. Sid James was gracing the Empire in a comedy called *The Mating Game*. During the show, he collapsed, and knowing what a prankster he was, his co-star continued ad-libbing for a while thinking he'd just gone off script. The audience thought this was all part of the show and were having a great time. When the curtain came down and someone called out the addled cliché 'is there a doctor in the house?' it was greeted with uproarious laughter. Sid was rushed to hospital, where he sadly died. The manager of the Empire at the time, Roy Todds, called the show's producer, Bill Roberton, to tell him what had happened. Roberton, also thinking it was a joke, replied with 'Don't worry, everybody dies in Sunderland.'

Flash forward to more recent history and the Sunderland Empire had a makeover that would change everything. In 2004 it had the height of its fly tower increased, a new (flat) stage and technical improvements that meant it would be able to stage larger productions. In fact, it would mean it was the only theatre between Manchester and Scotland that could host big West End productions, which have become its bread and butter.

The Sunderland Empire from the stage, looking right.

The Sunderland Empire from the stage.

The Empire Theatre main entrance, 2018.

A few years ago, Terpsichore (the fibreglass version) was damaged in high winds, and after hanging precariously from the roof of the Empire for several days was removed. It was feared that a new statue would have to be created, but thankfully it was able to be repaired. It took just under a year to get her back into place, during which time she was greatly missed by the people of Sunderland. In 2017 the Empire saw its latest refurbishment, with a bistro added and some cosmetic repairs. With all the refurbishments, the Empire at times can seem a bit like 'Trigger's broom', but many of the original features remain the same. The Sunderland Empire is the jewel in Sunderland's crown, and Terpsichore a beacon on the skyline, pulling in audiences from all over the country to enjoy a show and become a small part of its history.

DID YOU KNOW?
In 1990, Sunderland football club lost to Swindon Town 1-0 in play-offs, losing a place in the top tier. Unfortunately for Swindon, their chairman at the time was charged with thirty-six counts of improper conduct, including pay offs! Sunderland replaced them in the league, but the euphoria didn't last long as they were promptly relegated again the next season.

The Roker Roar

If you're a fan of Sunderland's football club, you'll have heard tales of the legend of the Roker Roar. If you're old enough, cast your mind back to those hazy, rose-coloured days of 1973, when Sunderland won the FA cup against Leeds United.

According to the club, the morning after that most triumphant victory, a journalist from London was spotted wandering around the grounds of Roker Park. A groundskeeper approached him and asked what he was up to.

> I've been reporting on top-class football all my life but I've never heard noise like that. It's a marvellous gimmick - where are the hidden amplifiers? (Sunderland AFC)

The groundskeeper was aghast and gave the journalist short shrift:

> There's no bloody amplifiers here mate. What you heard last night was the Roker Roar! (Sunderland AFC)

Sunderland supporters don't just raise the roof at their home ground either. When I interviewed former Sunderland AFC Chairman Sir Bob Murray in 2016, he waxed lyrical about the fans and the support they give to their club:

Queues at Roker Park. (Sunderland AFC)

When things are going well here, the noise in that stadium is scary. I was at Wembley when we played Manchester City the other week and I know the people at Wembley; I used to be on the board, well when our goal went in, they said that was the loudest roar they'd heard since new Wembley was opened. (Excerpt from *Sunderland, Industrial Giant*)

While Stadium of Light Roar doesn't have quite the same alliterative satisfaction as Roker Roar, there's no doubt that the fans of SAFC are some of the best and most supportive in the world. Currently nursing bruised egos from a double relegation into League One, the club have never needed that support more!

To Infinity and Beyond – the Space Clause

When hiring a new football player, you can probably imagine that them heading off into space is the last thing on the manager's mind. Not so in 1999, when Swedish footballer Stefan Schwarz was signed by Sunderland. Looking upon the dawn of a brand-new millennium, space exploration was still very much at fever pitch. The space shuttle Discovery docked with the International Space Station, Columbia blasted off, taking gold dollars into space with it, and the world waited eagerly as the Mars Polar Lander arrived at its destination. Large commercial companies had started to float the idea that space tourism might become a possibility, and, in fact, were already asking people to secure their flights for 2002. Schwarz had a huge interest in space travel and had apparently asked one of his advisors to book him on what would be the very first passenger space flight. Worried that this might affect his performance, SAFC added a clause into his contract stating he couldn't go into space and if he did, he'd be fired. Well, space flights for the general public didn't become a reality, but Stefan retired before 2002 in any case, feet still firmly on the ground.

DID YOU KNOW?
Many Sunderland residents have a bit of the old Roker Park ground in their houses. Closing in 1997, items were later auctioned off. Former chairman of the club Sir Bob Murray bought some turf, and he wasn't the only one. Supporter Chris O'Hara snapped some up too, a spot where his bins now stand, he jokes that maybe that's why the club is rubbish. Steven Rafferty's son bought seats from the Clock Stand that are now used in his garden, and Paula Hudson has the bar from the Player's Lounge – complete with footballer Eric Gates' chewing gum stuck underneath!

Hendon Board School and the Beginning of SAFC

If you're a resident of Sunderland or one of its nearby conurbations, it's an unwritten law that you have to support the football club.

Nobody can quite agree on exactly when Sunderland AFC started, but we do know that it all began with a chap called James Allan, a school teacher. Allan moved from Scotland to be headmaster at Hendon Board School in 1879. Imagine his surprise and distaste to find we were mostly playing rugby at that time, rather than 'Association Football', which he'd frequently played when in Glasgow. Trying to convert the town to his round ball ways, he brought a football (soccer ball, if you like) back from Scotland after popping back for a holiday. Keen for a kickabout, he rounded up friends and workmates and tried to get them interested in the game. There weren't too many colleagues to choose from – most teachers available to him at that time were women – but a pupil teacher called John Grayston was soon roped in.

> Though all the memories of later and more scintillating years may come between, my clearest memory is of my first game in the play yard. John Grayston (SAFC.com)

As Allan got his makeshift team together, they started to think about playing against others, somewhat reluctantly as it was difficult to commit to training while working and having busy lives. Towards the end of 1880, an advert was posted in *Athletic News* encouraging people to sign up for the Northumberland and Durham Cup before the deadline. This spurred on the team and they decided to commit. Their first competitive game was against Ferryhill Athletic, where they wore striking all blue and lost 1-0.

A souvenir card from 1890.
(Sunderland AFC)

   While we can say with relative certainty the team was formed somewhere between the original meeting they had in late 1879 and late 1880 when they signed up for their first official match, what were they called? They weren't SAFC as we know them now, and it seems there are references to more than one team name: the Sunderland and District Teachers' Association Football Club and the Sunderland School Teachers' Association Football Club. Let's be honest, they're not vastly different. After a year of this, they allowed non-teachers to join and so the name of the club was changed to Sunderland Association Football Club. They played at Blue House Field in Hendon for a while, and then moved around Sunderland before settling on Newcastle Road in 1886 in what was technically their first 'proper' ground. By this time, the team had won the Durham Senior Cup, but infighting was about to put it all in serious jeopardy. The club turned professional in 1887 and James Allan left – with many of his teammates – to form a rival club, Sunderland Albion. As is almost exclusively the way, the two local teams became bitter rivals and the town couldn't support both. Tom Watson became Sunderland AFC's manager in 1888 and just two years later William McGregor, the founder of the Football League, referred to SAFC as 'the team of all talents', which pretty much spelled the end for our friends at Sunderland Albion. SAFC moved to Roker Park in 1898 where they stayed, rather annoyingly, for ninety-nine years.

   Things were going pretty well: the team stayed in the First Division for sixty-eight years, won six league titles and broke a number of records. As footballing legends came and went, so too did two world wars, with Sunderland lads picking up where they left off if they were lucky enough to make it home unscathed. In 1958 Sunderland slipped out of the top tier for the first time, returning six years later in '64. The return to glory was not to last, and they bounced between the top two tiers for a while.

The opening of Roker Park, 1898. (Sunderland AFC)

The 1903 team with shield. (Sunderland AFC)

Managers took their turn, Roker Park gave way to its grander replacement, the Stadium of Light, and Sunderland managed to hang on to its position in the (now) Premier League ... for a little while at least. In May 2017 the club slipped down into the Championship, where it just couldn't find a toehold, tumbling into League One the following season, where it currently resides, dreaming of better days and playing against teams like Wycombe Wanderers and Scunthorpe United in a stadium built for Premier League crowds. As disheartening as this slide into mediocrity has been for many SAFC fans, they've stuck with their team, getting behind them in the hope that they can make that steady climb into the top flight once again. In some ways, where they are now is closer to their roots at Hendon Board School than they've been, almost since inception, and maybe the humility gained from such a fall from grace can help the team get back to its former glory.

3. Eclectic Survivors

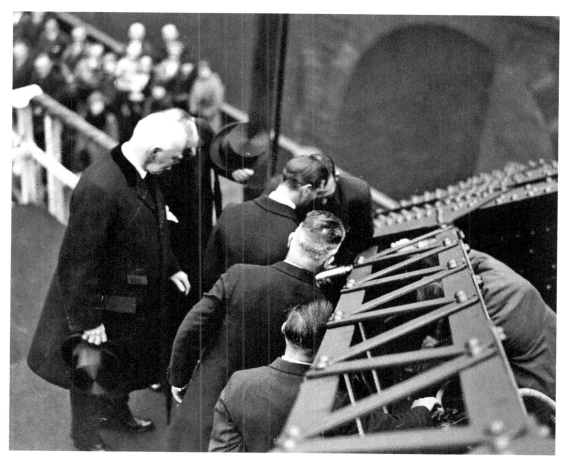

The Duke of York placing the final rivet (made out of silver) during the opening ceremony for the bridge on 31 October 1929. (Sunderland Museum and Winter Gardens)

Acoustic Mirror

Acoustic mirrors, or sound mirrors, are objects used to concentrate sound waves so that you can hear noise from a distance. Huge concrete structures, acoustic mirrors are concave like a satellite dish, and before radar they were used as an early warning device to detect incoming aircraft. Sound was reflected to a microphone placed in front of the dish with the idea being that the operator could then warn authorities of approaching danger. With mirrors set up around Britain, the clever bods monitoring them were able to work out the position of enemies in the sky, and this plotting of planes was able to help early teams develop radar.

Primarily, these mirrors were built on the north-east coast and the south coast from 1916 until the 1930s, when radar was invented. Unfortunately, the speed of technology quickly rendered the mirrors inadequate; by the time newer aircraft were approaching and were heard, there wasn't enough time to give warning.

What does all of this have to do with Sunderland? If you go down to Fulwell and pass the newly restored and picture-perfect windmill, keep heading past the car garage and take a left up a narrow little road, you'll eventually come to Sunderland's own acoustic mirror. Built in 1917 after a Zeppelin raid the year before, it was left to crumble, hidden by uncontrolled plant growth. It was placed on the Heritage England 'at risk' register and

The restored First World War acoustic mirror, Fulwell.

in 2013 a project to restore it to its former glory was given funding. Two years and almost £70,000 later, it was unveiled, complete with shiny new information panel. It is one of only a handful of acoustic mirrors remaining, and is one of only ten Sunderland structures included in the Schedule of Monuments, one of the oldest forms of heritage protection.

Cretehawser – the Concrete Boat

If you go down to the riverside at Claxheugh Rock (pronounced 'Clatchy' locally) in South Hylton, and the tide is just right, you might see an interesting lump of concrete shaped like a boat sticking up from the water. It may not look like much, but this is an interesting part of Sunderland's history. You'd be forgiven for wondering if this was an art installation; after all, a concrete boat?

To understand why, we have to go back in time a little to the end of the First World War. The war was a huge drain on resources, and raw materials had been siphoned off over the four years of conflict meaning that once the world returned to 'normal' these materials were scarce, so both here, and in the United States, shipbuilders looked towards a temporary solution: concrete. One of the potential issues with this was that traditional shipbuilders weren't used to building with concrete, but the government was offering a lucrative programme for those who could fulfil the demand for the new boats, and so a new company was formed.

Cretehawser, the concrete boat.

A close-up of *Cretehawser* at low tide.

Cretehawser, the name of the tug boat in question, was built by the Wear Concrete Building Company in Southwick, who were part of larger shipbuilders, Swan Hunter. It was launched in 1919, the first of an order of eight tug boats. It was thought and hoped that concrete would be a cheap material to build with, but they actually turned out to be considerably more expensive than their steel counterparts, costing almost 40 per cent more on average to make. As a result, the eight-tug order was reduced by the Ministry of Shipping, and the programme eventually scrapped.

Some of the concrete tugs that had made it to fruition had short but eventful lives: *Creterock* crashed into a trawler, *Cretecable* ran aground and *Creterope* was dismantled. So what of *Cretehawser*? She ticked along in use as a tug until 1935, after which she was sold for scrap to the South Stockton Shipping Company Ltd. The remains (the 'hulk') were sold back to Sunderland, this time to the River Wear Commissioners, who moored her in the South Dock to use as an emergency breakwater.

Cretehawser was hit in an air raid during the Second World War, so she was towed up river to her current spot, near to where she was built. The council considered moving her during a redevelopment of the riverbank, but it was decided she was an important part of Sunderland's heritage and left as a reminder of our short dabble into concrete boats.

DID YOU KNOW?
Big Ben – the name of the bell rather than the clock tower – in London – was cast in Stockton in 1856, but the clapper, or tongue, was made by George Hopper of Houghton-le-Spring. The bell actually cracked during regular testing and had to be broken up and melted down to be recast into a 'new' (young) Big Ben.

Gun Emplacement Benches

Roker is a pretty area of Sunderland, with its clean sandy beach and two lighthouses – one of which is now in retirement on the green at Cliff Park. Recently developed, it's the perfect spot to head to on a day out and enjoy one of the brand-new restaurants or just to enjoy the fresh sea air.

It's hard to imagine that from the eighteenth century up until 1922, Roker had (on and off) a gun battery. It began with four guns that got an upgrade every now and then, but they were still the rather outdated muzzle-loading types. In 1902 the guns were removed completely, but the necessity of defence in the First World War saw them reinstated in 1916, this time two 4.7-inch navel guns and a couple of searchlights. Gunners here fired at the Zeppelin that raided the town in April 1916.

After the war, the guns were removed and the battery was essentially abandoned in 1922. Another war was just around the corner though, and in 1940, as the Second World War progressed, 6-inch guns were installed, designed to be able to hit aircraft during air raids, as Sunderland was at considerable risk, being an industrial town.

The guns were once again taken away, and we might be forgiven for looking at the landscape now and never realising they were there, except for the placement of some benches along the cliff top. The distinctive semicircle shape and concrete wall that the benches are up against mark out the shape of the old battery. Next time you're enjoying

Gun emplacement benches at Roker.

an ice cream while sat on one of those benches, take a closer look. The circle of grass in the middle is where the gun would have stood, and the semicircle of wall protecting you from the cool snap of the sea breeze is the turning arc of the gun.

DID YOU KNOW?
Sunderland nearly missed out on a Vulcan because the call came on 1 April! John Stelling, Trustee at North East Land Sea and Air Museums (NELSAM) remembers: 'I received a call from Sunderland Airport that the RAF were bringing a Vulcan up and needed to see it was feasible to land. I had no knowledge of this and suspected it was a prank. Many calls later, we got confirmation and the Vulcan arrived on an inspection run, making two passes in front of the gathered crowd. Then Argentina invaded the Falklands, the Vulcans were needed and it was put on hold!'

A Vulcan aircraft at the North East Land Sea and Air Museums.

Codex Amiatinus

Religion might not be the first thing that leaps to mind when you think of Sunderland, but the links are strong. In the middle of the seventh century, Benedict Biscop built a monastery on the northern bank of the River Wear. The monastery was split over two sites, Monkwearmouth and Jarrow.

In the early eighth century, under the direction of Abbot Ceolfrith, the monks produced three bibles: one for Wearmouth, one for Jarrow and one – the Codex Amiatinus – to be taken as a gift for Pope Gregory II.

The Codex Amiatinus was half a metre high, written in Latin, and contained over 2,000 pages of vellum, for which an estimated 515 calf hides were required.

Travelling with a book of this size was an arduous task, but in AD 716, Abbot Ceolfrith left for Rome. Unfortunately, his was not to be a successful journey, and the abbot died in Burgundy, France, while en route. His followers continued his pilgrimage and took the book to Rome. From here, we lose track of the Codex Amiatinus and its two companions. Parts of the other two have turned up in a number of places, including at a property owned by the National Trust, and in a junk shop in Newcastle. The Codex Amiatinus, the last remaining version, popped up again in San Salvatore in Italy in the ninth century. For a while, it was believed that it was made by Italians, as the dedication page had been altered, and it wasn't until the nineteenth century that its true origin was revealed and Wearmouth-Jarrow received its dues.

Now the oldest surviving complete Latin bible in existence, and unusual in that it combines both old and new testament, the Codex Amiatinus has its home far from its north-east origins, in the Laurentian Library, Florence.

From the Codex Amiatinus: portrait of Ezra, from folio 5r at the start of the Old Testament.

4. Macabre Moments

Victoria Hall Stampede

On 16 June 1883, children of Sunderland gathered in excited anticipation for a variety show at the Victoria Hall. Designed by G. G. Hoskins, the hall was an impressive Gothic-style building that had opened eleven years earlier. Built to host meetings and as an entertainment venue, the most publicised event in its lifetime was also the one that would guarantee its place in the history books.

Tickets to see magician Alexander Fay were in the form of a flyer, promising entry for a penny. Children didn't need to produce the advert to gain access and so around 2,000 children (many more than the seating catered for) entered the Victoria Hall that day, enticed by the promise of magic tricks, marionettes and free toys. The show came and went without incident, until the end.

It was announced that gifts would be given out to certain ticket numbers upon exit. Performers began to distribute toys and books to the children in the stalls, and worried that they might miss out, the children seated further back began to surge down the stairs towards the door. It was at this point that events took a tragic turn. The exit door opened inward, and had been bolted so that it was only wide enough to fit one child through at a time.

> Children were tumbled head over heels, one on top of the other. Shrieks and screams vibrated through the staircase. More pressed down from above, inconsiderate of what might happen from this thoughtlessness. Accordingly, the children at the bottom of the stairs got packed, as it were, in a well. The heap of writhing and rolling humanity

The Victoria Hall prior to the disaster. (Sunderland Museum and Winter Gardens)

became higher and higher until it rose above the heads of those who were first jammed in the doorway and became a mass of struggling and dying children over six feet in height. (*Sunderland Echo*)

As events unfolded, a building that moments earlier was filled with laughter and chatter now pierced the air with cries and screams. The few adults in the building attempted to open the door, but with the bolt on the children's side, their efforts were in vein. Caretaker Frederick Graham rushed to another staircase and directed hundreds of children to safety through a different exit. Back at the bolted door, adults were attempting to pull children through the gap one at a time, until finally one man was able to pull the door from its hinges. For 183 children, it was too late; they had been crushed or suffocated in the rush to escape and ensuing panic.

William Codling, who was seven at the time of the incident, had attended with his sister Sarah:

I raced up the gallery as fast as I could, scrambled with the crowd through the doorway and jolted my way down two flights of stairs. Here the crowd was so compressed that there was no more racing but we moved forward together, shoulder to shoulder. Soon we were most uncomfortably packed but still going down. Suddenly I felt that I was treading upon someone lying on the stairs and I cried in horror to those behind 'Keep back, keep back! There's someone down'. It was no use, I passed slowly over and onwards with the mass and before long I passed over others without emotion. (Remembrances of the Victoria Hall Disaster 1883)

In the aftermath, the dead were laid out for parents to identify and it was reported that one little girl was seen carrying the body of her dead sister home.

Sunderland grieved for its lost children and the country mourned with it. Queen Victoria sent condolences to the bereaved families and donations of £5,000 were collected

Some of the Victoria Hall disaster victims' graves in Bishopwearmouth cemetery.

The Sunderland Calamity.

2OO CHILDREN CRUSHED TO DEATH,

IN THE VICTORIA HALL, ON SATURDAY, JUNE 16TH, 1883.

A WAIL of deep sorrow thrills over the land,
And scatters distraction on every hand;
Poor fathers and mothers their hearts have been wrung,
And bitter lament bursts from every tongue.

But a few short hours and children dear,
Who had just left their homes, without thought or fear,
In simple desire for childish joys,
Had gathered in hopes of the fatal toys.

A thousand poor things—little darlings all—
Were gathered within the Victoria Hall,
So happy they looked—'twas a charming sight—
To behold how they chattered and laughed with delight.

But who would have thought that this sight could have been
So suddenly changed to a terrible scene;
That dear little forms could, almost in a breath,
Have been crushed in their smiles by a horrible death.

Onward they rushed with impatience and glee,
Nor dreamt of the holocaust soon they would be,
Alas on each other they pressed to the door,
And knew not they'd see their dear parents no more.

They fell on each other a terrible heap,
A mass of crush'd forms in that staircase so deep,
And frantically struggling they fearfully cry—
For father or mother, then sinking they die.

Oh mothers of Sunderland wail for each child,
Rush madly to rescue in agony wild.
Oh fathers your hearts will be wrung when you hear
What a death has befallen the child you loved dear.

Strong arms soon were ready and willing to save,
But alas! near TWO HUNDRED must sleep in the grave,
And the voices of parents distracted with fears,
Cried aloud in the depth of their anguish and tears.

Oh look on the face of that dear little boy,
Or that sweet little girl, of some mother the joy,
Or that group of dear children some father's great pride,
Hand in hand they did go, now they lie side by side.

There's sorrow to-day in the town on the Wear,
There's grief for the loss of its children so dear;
And fathers and mothers must smother their pain,
For they know that they'll ne'er see their children again.

Oh! merciful Jesus, so loving and mild,
Receive in thy bosom each dear little child.
Oh! succour the suffering and soothe all their pain,
And comfort the heart of each parent again.

We thank thee, O Lord, for the children that's saved,
May the mem'ry of this on our hearts be engraved;
O'er the forms of the dear ones who sleep with the dead,
Sad tear-sprinkled wreaths of sweet flowers we'll spread.

Her Majesty, moved by a womanly love,
Her care for our little ones kindly did prove,
And many a mother's heart, stricken and sad,
Her message would comfort, though could not make glad.

J. H.

Newcastle-upon-Tyne: Published by ALLAN, Bookseller, 62, Dean Street, 28, Collingwood Street, and 18, Blackett Street.

A poem published shortly after the Victoria Hall disaster. (Sunderland Museum and Winter Gardens)

Grave of John Howard, aged six, who died
in the Victoria Hall stampede.

The Victoria Hall with the newly added memorial in the foreground. (Sunderland Museum and
Winter Gardens)

The memorial to the Victoria Hall disaster, Mowbray Park, 2018.

from people all over Britain, some of which was used for a memorial dedicated to the disaster: a grieving mother holding a dead child. The memorial, originally in Mowbray Park, moved to Bishopwearmouth Cemetery where many of the children were buried, but after falling into disrepair and being vandalised, it was restored and in 2002 returned to the park.

As well documented as the Victoria Hall stampede was, the events that unfolded on 16 June 1883 caused a national outcry. An inquiry couldn't identify who was responsible for bolting the door and so nobody was prosecuted. It did, however, lead to legislation whereby public venues must have a minimum number of outward opening exits, which in turn led to the invention of the push-bar emergency exits we all recognise today.

Sunderland was the first to implement the policy, with its children's mission on Prospect Row. A blue plaque, part of the 'Old Sunderland Heritage Trail', marks this historic change.

Cholera – a Plague Comes to Sunderland

Cholera, or cholera morbus as it was known then to distinguish it from other strains, was first noticed and described by British troops in India in 1817 and spread through trade routes.

Although not necessarily a serious disease, treatment of the time usually called for a restriction of fluids and the prescription of purgatives to try and flush the system – the opposite of what the body needed to recover from the sickness and diarrhoea that were brought on by cholera.

CHOLERA MORBUS.

TO THE

PUBLIC.

IN justice to the Community, and also to myself, I find it needful to publish the following Facts, which I dare any Man, or set of Men to disprove.

When the Board of Health of this Town was first established, I was called to the Chair of the Medical Department, and many salutary Plans and Regulations were from time to time discussed at our Medical Meetings.

On Tuesday the 1st. of November, at a General Meeting of the Medical Department of the Board of Health, at which all the Members of the Board were invited, I understand the following Medical Gentlemen were present. I give them as far as I am able, according to Seniority: Doctors Clanny, Miller, Atkinson, Brown, Haslewood, Burn, Happer, Ogden, and Croudace—Surgeons, Happer, Croudace, Fothergill, Dixon, Smithson, Holmes, Torbock, Embleton, Cooke, Penman, Mordey, and Maling. Five Cases of Cholera were reported, of which, Four had died in a few days, and the Fifth being at the Point of Death. The following Query was put from the Chair, without comment.

Is it the Opinion of the Medical Gentlemen present, that we have the Continental Cholera amongst us? Those who are of this Opinion will hold up their Hands, when it was carried unanimously. Next, those who are of a contrary opinion, will hold up their hands, when not one Hand was held up.

A General Meeting of the *Board of Health*, was convened soon afterwards, and the following Resolution was drawn up by DR. BROWN, and agreed to unanimously.

"Resolved, that the Medical Gentlemen, under whose Observation Cases of C. Cholera have fallen, draw up a full Report of them, and place them, by the Forenoon of the 2nd. instant, in the Hands of Dr. Clanny, to be transmitted by him to the Board of Health of London."

This Report arrived in London on the 4th of November, when the Privy Council immediately ordered the Town of Sunderland to be placed in Quarantine.

As is the Duty of a Chairman I did not vote, nor could I, except a casting Vote had been needful.

These Facts remove from me the Odium, which some designing and ill-informed Men have propogated; and for these Facts, I have the original Documents in my possession. As the Organ of the Medical Department of the Board of Health of Sunderland, I have faith fully discharged my Duty between God and Man, and what I have performed has been barely Official, as Chairman of the Medical Department of the Board.

W. REID CLANNY, M. D.

Saturday Night, Nov. 12th, 1831.

H. J. Dixon, Printer, High Street, Bishopwearmouth.

A poster warning of cholera morbus, 1831. (Sunderland Museum and Winter Gardens)

A drawing showing 'blue stage cholera', 1831. (Sunderland Museum and Winter Gardens)

A list of cholera victims from 1866. (Sunderland Museum and Winter Gardens)

Holy Trinity Church, the site
of a mass cholera grave.

As it spread, people became aware of its high mortality rate, and governments started to implement measures to stop the progression. By 1823, cholera was in Russia and any ships from the Baltic states coming to England were put under quarantine. Unfortunately, in October of 1831, the port authorities at Sunderland decided to ignore these instructions and allow a ship to dock.

William Sproat was the first officially recorded victim of cholera in England. By late December it had reached Gateshead and by January 1832 London. In February of the same year, Parliament passed the Cholera Morbus Prevention Act but the country was already in the grip of an epidemic. Between 1831 and 1832, 32,000 people died, over 200 of them in Sunderland.

Even with the large number of deaths, very little changed in order to stop the same thing happening again, so sure enough it did. Another pandemic hit the UK in 1848 with a further 62,000 deaths. As a result of this, the Public Health Act of 1848 was passed, ensuring improvements to drainage, clean drinking water and the setting up of local Boards of Health.

DID YOU KNOW?
Most of us have heard about when the sixteenth US President, Abraham Lincoln, was assassinated in 1865 at the theatre. What fewer people know is that Lincoln was watching a farce called 'Our American Cousin', which was written by Sunderland-born Tom Taylor. Tom would go on to write over seventy-five pieces, but unsurprisingly none were more popular than the play that turned out to be Lincoln's last!

Sunderland Bombardment – the First World War Comes to Sunderland
In December of 1914, Germany tried to draw out elements of the Royal Navy by attacking Hartlepool (along with Scarborough and Whitby), killing over 100 people. The Hartlepool

Bombardment is well documented, but many aren't as aware that Sunderland was the target for two attacks, one planned, and one accidental, just two years later.

On 1 April 1916 at around 10 p.m., German Imperial Navy Zeppelin L11 set out to attack England. Although L11 was trying to reach central or southern England, strong winds pushed it off course to the north. Not wanting to waste an opportunity, the commander of L11 decided to hit key targets on the coast, including the Port of Sunderland. Around 11 p.m., several bombs and incendiaries were dropped overboard, with more than 100 people injured and twenty losing their lives. Roads, houses and trams were destroyed, and the Goods Yard and railway station were badly damaged, but due to wartime censorship, the full account of the raid wasn't reported until years later.

In France, the Battle of the Somme was approaching and on the 1 July 1916, the first day of the battle, the loss of life was enormous. Britain suffered almost 20,000 fatalities and nearly 60,000 wounded, for nominal advancement. At this point, telegrams informing families of the tragic news would have been flooding in to Sunderland.

During the Battle of Jutland, the Germans tried a similar technique to the Hartlepool bombardment, of luring out their opposition with the intention of trapping and destroying the fleet. This had mixed results, and both sides claimed victory – the British ultimately lost more ships and people, but managed to contain the German fleet – and so

District No.

In the Event of a
Bombardment of Sunderland.

Generally speaking, it is safer indoors than in the streets. If indoors, select the room furthest from the sea, and, if suitable, in the lowest part of the house, and remain there.

THE FOLLOWING MAY BE USEFUL:—

A strong table covered with mattresses, etc., could be used as a shelter from splinters, bricks, etc. Water, candles, matches and food ready at hand. Gas meter turned off.

If you have no suitable shelter, then make for the open country
Via Moran Street, down the Dene,
keeping away from houses wherever possible.

—— o ——

Special Constable for..............................Street

Mr...

Mr...

INGRAM E. PEACE,
SOUTHWICK PRINTING WORKS.

Directions in the event of a bombardment. (Sunderland Museum and Winter Gardens)

the remaining British fleet were forced to stay in the North Sea to keep the Germans from getting to the United Kingdom.

Still reeling from the Zeppelin attack and the terrible news of the Battle of the Somme, just a couple of months later, in August 1916 more bad news was heading to the people of Sunderland. German commander Admiral Reinhard Scheer had hatched a plan to bombard the town to keep up momentum and morale after Jutland. If it succeeded, the results would be devastating to the area, just as with the Hartlepool Bombardment and Sunderland Zeppelin raid. What the Germans didn't know was the British Intelligence had intercepted and decoded radio messages and so were well aware that an attack was on the horizon. Ships were sent out to be stationed in areas that the Germans were likely to arrive. In yet another twist, a German Zeppelin, L13, had spotted the shifting British fleet and warned their comrades. Scheer turned and headed for home, abandoning his target, and so Sunderland was spared a potential tragedy.

Sunderland Blitz – the Second World War Comes to Sunderland

Sunderland got off relatively lightly in terms of being bombed during the First World War, but by the time the Second World War had really got going, they wouldn't be so lucky. In June 1940, the Germans started their bombing of Great Britain, known as the Blitz. When we think of the Blitz it's easy to just give thought to London. We've all seen the images of well-known streets and landmarks reduced to rubble, but in fact the North East was significantly bombed due to it being a hive of industrial activity.

15 August 1940, No. 48 Atkinson Road, H.E. bomb, no casualties. (Sunderland Local Studies Library)

Sunderland was a vital shipbuilding town and so the Germans had planned to attack it strategically, destroying vital yards, associated industry and transport links like the railway, and its bridges.

Dropping bombs wasn't really an accurate science and they could easily be blown off target or even just dropped in the wrong place mistakenly if visibility was poor. The Germans did succeed in creating a great deal of damage and chaos in Sunderland, though. The railway station was successfully hit, the Victoria Hall was destroyed – as was the Winter Gardens, by the same blast – and many streets, houses and churches were damaged in explosions. May 1943 was one of the worst months with a staggering number of bombs dropped each day:

On the night of 15–16 of the month, an estimated sixty-seven bombers unloaded 127 tons of bombs and 1,300 incendiaries over Sunderland, causing extensive damage and killing sixty-nine people. On the night of 23–24 May, sixty-two bombers made the final major raid and Sunderland was again the principle objective. Ten parachute mines, ninety-two high explosives and thousands of incendiaries caused widespread destruction of lives and property. Eighty-four people died in the attack. (*Luftwaffe Losses Over Northumberland and Durham 1939–1945* by Bill Norman)

6 September 1940, Union Street. Two pairs of carriage wheels thrown through roof of station. No casualties. (Sunderland Local Studies Library)

It's hard to imagine how the town must have felt during those years, not knowing whether their sleep would be pierced by the sound of an air-raid siren or whether their houses would still be there when they got back from the bomb shelter.

> During an alert that lasted from 11 p.m. until 4 a.m. the area around my grandfather's house was hit by 3 heavy bombs, which destroyed 25 houses and killed 13 neighbours. You can imagine the fear and anxiety that my grandparents suffered. I was meanwhile considered fairly safe in my uncle's house. That was until 2 days later a huge landmine landed by parachute in his street about 20 yards from his front door! Luckily for all of us it did not explode but lay in a big hole in the road until a brave army bomb squad defused it. If this mine had exploded many surrounding homes would have been destroyed and many families including our own would certainly have been killed. After this incident Jerry left us alone for a while to concentrate his bombers on the eastern front. (Malcolm Henry Nolan from WW2 People's War – BBC)

Nearly 7, 000 people in the North East were killed during bombing in the Second World War. While it might seem confined to the pages of history and the black and white photographs we see in museums, you just have to look around Sunderland to see a tiny glimpse into that time. The Winter Gardens was rebuilt (but not until much later), and

10 April 1941, Binns Ltd, Fawcett Street. Fire caused by a large number of incendiary bombs. East side of premises gutted. No casualties. (Sunderland Local Studies Library)

16 May 1943. One firepot bomb fell at the centre of Farnham Terrace and Chester Road and failed to explode. Bomb disposal squad pictured. (Sunderland Local Studies Library)

The Bridges shopping centre, the former site of The Empress Hotel.

where the Victoria Hall once stood – a grand and imposing building – is now a rather less glamourous insurance office and car park. The Empress Hotel was reduced to rubble, and soon after a makeshift market developed, with people selling their wares on the site. You might say that site has kept some of its wartime spirit, as now, on that land, is our covered shopping mall, The Bridges.

Resurrection Men and Half-hanged Jack

Edinburgh in the early 1800s was a frontrunner in the field of medical science. Medical students need cadavers on which to practice, but these were in short supply at the time. The law stated that they could only use bodies where the person had died in prison, had committed suicide or were orphans. With only around five bodies being allocated each year, doctors started looking at other ways they might obtain a corpse. With money to be made, bodysnatching thrived to the point where relatives would have burial sites watched for a while to make sure nobody could pinch Great Uncle Albert. Once the bodies had started to decompose, they were of no use to the doctors, and so, worthless to the snatchers who were quickly dubbed 'resurrection men'. Such was the demand, and the fear of a grave being robbed that high towers and walls were built around Edinburgh cemeteries, to keep the thieves out – or at least to make it difficult to get a body back out!

Sunderland was having its own issues with grave robbing, as was much of the country by now. The rector at the Holy Trinity Church in Hendon ordered a ditch to be dug, which in conjunction with the high walls, it was hoped would keep out these resurrectionists.

In 1827 William Burke and William Hare crossed paths in Edinburgh when Burke moved into a lodging house run by Hare. One of the other residents died while still owing money, and seeing an opportunity, they sold the body to Dr Robert Knox of Edinburgh College in order to reclaim what Hare believed he was owed. They weighed the man's coffin down with bark to avoid suspicion.

The two men were pleased by their earnings and the ease with which they'd managed the situation, and so when a tenant became ill, Burke and Hare hurried the process along by suffocating him in order to leave the body unmarked. This would later become known as 'Burking'.

More tenants were murdered, as were prostitutes and the old and infirm – anyone that Burke and Hare felt they could get away with killing. One woman had the misfortune to go looking for her mother (who the pair had already killed) and so she was added to their growing list of victims who were either smothered or strangled.

Sunderland loves a good claim to fame, even a grisly one, and there are rumours claiming Burke and Hare visited Sunderland to ply their trade. Dates put this at around 1824, which would seem unlikely if most records say they met a few years after that, but certainly Sunderland was targeted by bodysnatchers and it's not impossible that the most famous of the resurrectionists might have paid us a visit – it makes a fun story at the very least. One account tells of a man dubbed 'Half Hanged Jack' who attempted to prise a body from the ground at Holy Trinity by tying a noose around his horse. Unfortunately for him, the rope became tangled around his neck and he almost strangled himself before he was found.

Holy Trinity Church.

William Hare

William Burke

William Burke and William Hare.

Back in Edinburgh, there was eventually an argument between Burke and Hare about the latter cutting the former out of his deals with Knox. This led to Burke and his wife Helen taking in their own lodgers. They invited a woman called Marjory Campbell Docherty to stay and murdered her, telling the other lodgers – a couple called Ann and James Gray – that she'd been asked to leave. They were suspicious and on investigation discovered Marjory's body under one of the beds. Refusing an offer of a bribe, the Grays called the police.

When arrested, Burke, Hare and their wives all blamed each other and although an examination of Marjory's body showed that it was likely she had been suffocated, they'd managed to move the body to Knox before the police got there, so there was no actual proof of the crime. Hare was eventually offered immunity if he would testify against Burke, which he agreed to. Burke was sentenced to death by hanging, which happened in front of a crowd of over 25,000 in January 1829. There was not enough evidence to convict his wife. In a twist of irony, Burke's body was donated to medical science.

Hare, bafflingly, was released a month after Burke's hanging, and we don't know what happened to him. Rumour has it that he was blinded as a result of being thrown into a quarry by an angry mob. Dr Knox was cleared of any wrongdoing and eventually left Edinburgh to lecture around Britain and Europe. He was eventually debarred after breaking the rules, and lived out his life as a pathological anatomist at a cancer hospital before finally establishing his own practice in Hackney.

The Burke and Hare murders (and the subsequent murders by the London Burkers) led to a change in the law, The Anatomy Act 1832, whereby doctors and students would have increased access to cadavers and be allowed to have bodies legally donated to them, which put an end to the need for bodysnatching.

EXECUTION of the notorious WILLIAM BURKE the murderer, who supplied DᵣKNOX with subjects.

An etching of the execution of William Burke.

58

The Great Fire of Sunderland

The Great Fire of London is something most of us know a little about, and the Great Fire of Tyneside you might be aware of if you're up on your North East history; however, what many people don't know is that Sunderland had its own Great Fire.

By the late nineteenth century, Sunderland was a busy port town, a hive of activity, with shops and other businesses springing up in the centre of town around High Street and Fawcett Street. A large drapery, Havelock House, stood on the corner of Fawcett Street, opposite the grand Hutchinson's Buildings, more popularly known as Mackie's Corner after hatter Robert Mackie, who had a store there from 1850.

Havelock House fire, 1898. (Sunderland Local Studies Library)

The evening of 18 July 1898 was a breezy one. A fire started in Havelock House, and as the building was full of highly flammable materials it wasn't long before it was cloaked in flames. Wind fed the fire and helped it spread, and it leapt across the street as well as engulfing neighbouring buildings. Crowds gathered to spectate as police and firefighters rushed to the scene, and they weren't the only ones. Postal workers in the area stood in a line to create a barrier to prevent people from getting too close. While these brave souls put themselves in the path of danger, there were some less saintly Sunderland residents who were taking advantage of everyone's attention being drawn in one direction.

As the fire burned, these ne'er-do-wells broke windows of nearby shops and were stealing the wares! Donkin's music shop was one of those broken into, and as well as smaller instruments like trumpets, they also lost pianos, such was the effectiveness of the fire as a distraction. Some of the posties tackled a few thieves when they saw what was happening, and stored the stolen items in the post office until later.

Almost fifty premises were damaged or destroyed, but thankfully there was no loss of life. There would be, however, a considerable rebuilding of Sunderland centre. The damage totalled over £400, 000 – a staggering amount for that time. John Stott was tasked with rebuilding and within eighteen months had created a department store on the site of

Fire damage, 1898. (Sunderland Museum and Winter Gardens)

Havelock House and repaired the Hutchinson's Buildings, modifying them to match the rest of the street.

The severity of the fire and subsequent damage was cause for a serious rethink about the organisation of fire services. Up until then the police had been responsible, using parish fire engines, but seeing the devastating effects of the fire and the potential for tragedy that had narrowly been avoided, a separate fire brigade was created. Two steam fire engines were purchased and a new fire station was eventually built. That Edwardian station, which opened in 1907, closed in 1992 and lay unused for a number of years until it was restored and given a new lease of life as a restaurant and arts venue, which opened in November of 2017. Although no longer associated with the fire service, it's retained many of its original features, including the dramatic arches of the former fire appliance ports, and is truly one of Sunderland city centre's most striking features.

Mackie's Corner, 2018.

The former Sunderland Central Fire Station, now a restaurant, entertainment venue and 'culture hub'.

5. Buildings and Places

Sunderland Cottages

In the nineteenth century, industry was booming, and as a town that relied heavily on it, Sunderland was flooded with people seeking work. This created an unprecedented demand for housing and Sunderland just couldn't cope. 'In 1801 Sunderland's population stood at 12,412, but by 1831 it had risen to 17,060' (*A History of Sunderland*, Glen Dodds).

There weren't enough houses for all these new workers and many couldn't afford to live in middle-class developments like the Fawcett estate. Affordable housing was needed, and soon. The solution? Sunderland cottages, one-storey terraced houses that were thrown up quickly, row on row, in tight grids. Built close to places of industry like the shipyards and glassworks, these were perfect for the skilled workers coming into Sunderland: they were low cost, and even had an outside space in the form of a yard or a garden. This new design was no small thing, and it offered more privacy for families and started to shift social norms away from the more communal activities and way of living that had arisen from close-knit pit housing.

Sunderland Cottages, Francis
Street, 1974. (Sunderland
Museum and Winter Gardens)

It's likely that the inspiration for Sunderland cottages came from mining villages and their rows of pit cottages, a common sight on the Durham Coalfield. Indeed, the coal companies funded a number of these pit houses in Sunderland, as it was in their interests to encourage a stable workforce.

It wasn't actually the industry owners and managers who built these houses, at least not initially. Builders spotted the opportunity and seized it, building the houses speculatively. As demand grew, the coal company and Hartley's Glassworks in Millfield got on board, building eighty homes with a slight variation on the original – these included attic rooms.

As transport links improved and the tram system extended out into the suburbs, commuting to work became easier and so cottages started to be built away from the areas of heavy industry, closer to middle-class neighbourhoods. High Barnes is a good example of this, as are the ABC streets (named for their literal alphabetisation), which are still around today.

Building houses became another of Sunderland's important industries and by the early 1900s only shipbuilding was ahead of it in terms of employment. Owning your own house was an important part of a person's identity and pride, and ownership figures in Sunderland soared above those of the national average of 20 per cent to an enormous 80 per cent in Hendon. The creation of the cottages, in their various and evolving forms, continued up until the 1930s, almost 100 years after evidence suggests building started.

Derelict Cottages, Gordon Terrace, Southwick. (Sunderland Museum and Winter Gardens)

Gosforth Street showing
broken windows. (Sunderland
Museum and Winter Gardens)

Hendon Street, 1958.
(Sunderland Museum and
Winter Gardens)

Dunbar Street (of the ABC
streets), 2018.

Although probably not realised at the time, we now look back on the design and implementation of Sunderland cottages as a landmark period in its history. Not only did it solve a housing crisis in an inventive way, it got numerous workers away from slum living and into their own, respectable homes, which was a source of pride for many and a way to build on their social status.

When some of these houses started to be demolished in so-called slum clearances, there was outrage from the public and many letters written to the *Sunderland Echo* by residents in protest. Building preference was now leaning towards tower blocks, a shiny, modern dream of 'cities in the sky'.

Sunderland cottages were built to last and of those that survived the clearances, many fine examples are still around and lived in today, over a century and a half after their first inception. The owners can take pride in knowing that their home is a distinctive part of not only Sunderland's history, but of Britain's.

Sunderland Sikh Temple

Sunderland is a diverse city and in the heart of Ashbrooke you may spot a Christian church with the spire wrapped in yellow cloth.

Christ Church, built by James Murray between 1862 and 1864, was one of the oldest buildings in Sunderland. In need of desperate repair, the church was purchased in 2001 for just £1 by Sunderland Sikh Association, who raised the money needed to renovate it

Inside Guru Gobind Singh Gurdwara Sikh Centre.

Former Christ Church and the newly restored First World War memorial.

from members of their community. They took out the pews and alters, put down carpet, and added toilets, a heating system and new rooms. As well as making necessary changes like this, the Association were keen to save and restore important parts of the building's history and character, keeping many original features like the stained-glass windows and vaulted roof.

Now a congregation of up to 500 meet at the Guru Gobind Singh Gurdwara Sikh Centre (or Ashbrook Hall as it's often called) for a variety of events. As well as serving the Sikhs of the area, the centre has also helped with developing a bond between different communities: it facilitates school visits, opens its doors as part of Sunderland's Heritage Open Days, and invites residents to use its rooms for various interest groups and activities.

In 2017, the Association worked on restoring another important part of the church's history: a war memorial. Unveiled in 1921, it was erected in the grounds of the church to commemorate the sixty-seven men of the area who died during the First World War. Restoration took two weeks and the memorial was given a new lease of life for those who wish to pay their respects.

DID YOU KNOW?
If you wander around Sunderland's East End near to the Quayside Exchange, and cast your eyes upwards, you might spot a building topped with an eagle. It may not surprise you to learn that this building is known as the Eagle Building and it's one of Sunderland's oldest, formerly in use as an inn and coaching tavern. The original wooden eagle was taken down to protect it during the Second World War and it took sixty years for a replacement to be made. The original 7-foot eagle still exits, and lives in the owner's house in the Channel Islands.

The eagle atop the 'Eagle Building' in Sunderland's East End.

Washington Old Hall

Many are familiar with the links to the United States that the North East has, but Sunderland in particular has many ties. There's the Friendship Agreement with Washington DC, which started in 2006 and has seen a sharing of cultural heritage across the pond, and if you're a regular visitor to Washington (part of Sunderland since the '70s), then you can't help but notice its similarly named counterpart, Washington DC. In fact, our Washington was the original, coming from William De Hartburn, who changed his name to William De Washington (then known as Wessyngton, or Wassyngton) after buying the Manor of Washington.

Descendants of the manor, or Washington Old Hall as it came to be known, have links to the original US President and founding father George Washington. His ancestors lived there around the 1100s but most left around 1400 for places like Cumbria, where Washington's direct descendants settled.

In the early 1600s, the remaining Washington family left the area and so the hall was sold to the Bishop of Durham. In the later part of the eighteenth century, Washington Old Hall was used as tenement housing, accommodating up to thirty-five people in five bedrooms. In 1936 it was facing demolition after falling into disrepair, so a group of locals started a group to save the building and raise money for restoration. The Second World War caused the building work to be put on hold, but it resumed in 1951 and was completed in 1955 when it was officially opened by the American Ambassador. Much of the money donated was given by American benefactors who also contributed furniture. Due to the extensive remodelling of the hall, very little of the original layout remains, but donated portraits of George Washington and illustrations from the Independence era mean the connection to Washington is still very strong.

Wearside Masonic Temple

Funny handshakes and grand meeting halls may spring to mind if I asked you about the Freemasons. They're a male-centric organisation of over 200,000 people, and most famously they're shrouded in mystery.

The Freemasons are believed to come from medieval trade guilds, like stonemasons. As these people needed to travel a lot, they developed a language of handshakes, code phrases and symbols to help with recognition and to gain trust. Much of the symbolism is the same today, though there's no direct link.

Now, one of the main reasons people join the Freemasons is the camaraderie, helped by dinners at their lodges, usually grand buildings with long histories.

Phoenix Hall is a Grade I listed building in Queen Street East, Sunderland. Built in 1785 to replace a smaller lodge that had burned down, it is thought to be the oldest purpose-built Masonic meeting places still in use in the world.

DID YOU KNOW?
Roker Lighthouse housed a garrison in both world wars. It contained a torpedo battery, but this was never used. A soldier died here, not through an act of war but rather as the result of a tragic accident. The young man was carrying supplies through the pier tunnel when a wave crashed through the skylight and he was killed.

Phoenix Hall – Wearside Masonic Temple – 2018.

Sunderland Museum and Winter Gardens

After a few false starts, Sunderland Museum housed its collection in the Athenaeum Building when it opened in 1841. By the mid-1840s, it was taken over by the local authority and was the first municipally funded museum in the country outside of London, housing an impressive array of Sunderland produced pottery, particularly lusterware, which had a distinctive pink glaze. Its aim: 'for the instruction and amusement of the inhabitants of the borough'. Their very first acquisition, though, was a painting of the opening of the new South Dock that had been commissioned by the Sunderland Corporation.

In the 1870s, plans for a new museum, library, council offices and gardens were raised. After some objection and a little indecision, the foundation stone for the Museum and Winter Gardens was laid in Mowbray Park by Mayor Alderman Storey in 1877, attended by Ulysses S. Grant, whose term as President of the United States of America had only just come to an end. Two years later Sunderland Museum and Winter Gardens was officially opened at its new home next to Mowbray Park.

The museum housed a variety of interesting exhibits, many of which it still has today. These included a taxidermy lion named Wallace – who supposedly had mauled his tamer during a show in Sunderland; a walrus killed in Siberia, which is said to have been an inspiration for Lewis Carrol's poem 'The Walrus and the Carpenter', a Coelurosauravus fossil (a gliding reptile), which is over 250 million years old; and a large collection of the works L. S. Lowry.

The Winter Gardens, 2018.

In 1913, curator J. A. Charlton Deas started sessions at the museum that were designed for those with visual impairments. Adults and children alike were invited to the museum for a 'touch tour', where they could feel the taxidermy animals (like Wallace) and touch the various other shapes and textures of the exhibits. It was an important development in the museum world, and influenced similar events across the country.

Like many civic buildings in the Second World War, the Winter Gardens were damaged when a mine was dropped onto and destroyed the nearby Victoria Hall. What you may not know is that they were potentially being demolished anyway, after being deemed too small for their use. The gardens weren't immediately rebuilt; instead the land was used to extend the library and museum in the 1960s.

In 1995 the library moved to Fawcett Street as part of the City Library and Arts Centre (it's now back in the museum building), and at the turn of the new century a major refurbishment saw covered gardens return to the site once again, opening in 2001 and boasting some 2,000 different species of plants.

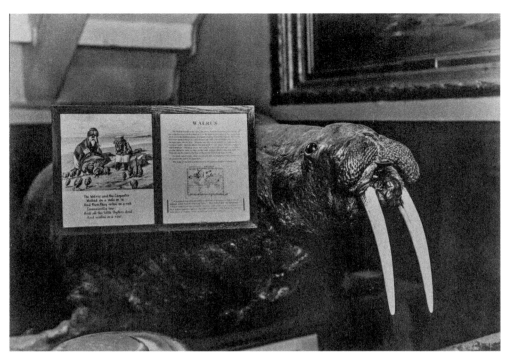

The famous walrus, said to have inspired Lewis Carrol. (Sunderland Museum and Winter Gardens)

Wallace the lion being visited by the blind as part of Deas' 'touch tour'. (Sunderland Museum and Winter Gardens)

Winter Gardens 'touch tour' visit by the
blind, organised by J. A. Charlton Deas.
(Sunderland Museum and Winter Gardens)

A statue in Mowbray Park based on the walrus exhibit. The Winter Gardens can be seen in the
background.

Hilton (now Hylton) Castle from a plate, 1 May 1817. (Sunderland Museum and Winter Gardens)

DID YOU KNOW?
Hylton Castle was originally a wooden structure built around 1066. It was rebuilt in stone around the early fifteenth century. It's said to be haunted by the Cauld Lad of Hylton, who is rumoured to be the ghost of a naked boy crying 'I'm cauld (cold)', and although reports vary as to his origin, it seems is legend comes from a boy that Baron Hylton killed, and for whose murder he was later pardoned.

Grindon Hall

In my lifetime, Grindon Hall has been a residential home, a private Christian school and more recently a non-selective school open to people of all faiths. As its name suggests, Grindon Hall was a manor house originally belonging to the Doxford family, but its history in between those two incarnations is the most interesting, when it was a sanatorium, primarily dealing with cases of tuberculosis and venereal diseases.

Tuberculosis had been a particularly dangerous disease in the past, given various monikers like 'consumption', 'the white plague' and my personal favourite 'the king's evil'. In the 1850s one in every four people who contracted it in Europe would die. Treatment at that time was bed rest in a sanatorium, with fresh air (in all weathers), a good diet and a 'wait-and-see' attitude. As medical advances progressed, treatment and more importantly prevention, got better.

Grindon Hall, date unknown, but probably around turn of the century – certainly pre-1920s. (Sunderland Local Studies Library)

Grindon Hall, 2018.

In the 1920s, around the time Grindon Hall was being purchased for use as a sanitorium, trials of the first vaccine for TB were taking place and conferences were being held around the world to raise awareness of the disease and discuss its treatment and prevention. At the end of the '20s, Alexander Fleming discovered the first antibiotic: penicillin. However, it took over a decade to see its true potential and start producing antibiotics en masse. With the vaccine for prevention and the development of antibiotics to not only help treat but speed recovery for those who did contract TB, cases started to slow. For a contagious disease, cutting down recovery time also means reducing the likelihood of others catching it and continuing the spread of the infection.

As tuberculosis became less of a problem in the western world and easier to contain, the need for sanatoriums dwindled, and Grindon Hall became part of the hospital(s), and eventually a residential home for people with difficulties. In the late '80s it became a school and has been ever since, with the hall building itself being used for the secondary school children, and the Grade II listed stables converted for use by the primary years.

6. Innovation, Industry and Invention

Joseph Swan and the Light Bulb

If you ask someone who invented the light bulb, very often the reply is 'Thomas Edison', and the core of Sunderland shakes with fury. In fact, Edison's light bulb was demonstrated in December 1879, but a chap called Joseph Swan had shown his in Fawcett Street in January of the same year, almost a full year earlier.

Joseph Swan was born in Sunderland in Pallion Hall in 1828. He was said to be an inquisitive child who read a lot, was always keen to learn, and even attended lectures at the Sunderland Athenaeum. He apprenticed at a pharmacy as a young teenager and later partnered with his friend John Mawson in a chemist manufacturing firm. It was here that he was inspired by two things: light and photography.

Swan and Mawson produced collodion, which is used in wet-plate photography, reducing the exposure time needed to make a photo. Heat increased the sensitivity of the

Joseph Swan. (Sunderland Museum and Winter Gardens)

emulsion used and so he developed dry plates that worked using glass, resulting in glass plate photography. He also patented bromide paper and the transfer process for carbon prints, meaning that lasting photographic prints could be created with a much larger tonal range.

Swan started to work on a light bulb in the mid-1850s, building on existing work by Volta and Humphry Davy, particularly the latter's arc lamp. By 1860 he'd developed a bulb that used a carbon paper filament (instead of platinum) in an evacuated glass bulb. Due to the lack of an adequate vacuum pump, though, the bulbs burned out quickly and were never very bright to start with, as higher temperatures meant a greater danger of combustion. He worked to create a better vacuum and used carbonised thread as a filament instead of paper, and so by 1875 he'd created a much better version that could burn brighter, for longer. This version, which he patented in Britain, was the one Swan demonstrated in lectures in 1878–79, including in Sunderland.

Thomas Edison. (Library of Congress)

In 1880, he formed the Swan Electric Light Company Ltd and patented a bulb that made use of cotton thread as a filament. By this time, Swan was living in Gateshead and his was the first home in the world to have electric lighting. Swan started to install his bulbs around the area, at popular locations like the Lit & Phil in Newcastle, which, in another first, was the first public building in the world to have electric lighting.

But what of Thomas Edison at this time? Well, Edison had been working on his own version of the bulb, trying to improve on Swan's original and was producing these under his own company, the Edison Electric Light Company. Edison had patented his version (later invalidated by the US patents office in 1883), but it came after Swan's, and so Swan took him to court. Edison lost and was forced to take Swan on as a partner. Swan and Edison merged their companies to form Edison and Swan United Electric Light Company, which was frequently known as 'Ediswan'. The company produced and sold the cellulose filament bulbs Swan had invented in 1881, variations of which led to the bulbs we use today.

Ediswan poster.
(Sunderland Museum and
Winter Gardens)

Lord Durham opens the Queen Alexandra Bridge, 1909. (Sunderland Museum and Winter Gardens)

While we can accurately say Thomas Edison produced the first commercially viable light bulb, one that lasted and was inexpensive, it's unfair to credit Edison with the invention of the bulb. Could he have achieved it without the groundwork laid by Swan? Well, who knows, but he didn't. Swan did, and Sunderland can claim him as one of their own with pride.

DID YOU KNOW?
When the Queen Alexandra Bridge was opened in 1909, it was the heaviest bridge in Britain. It cost almost half a million pounds, took two years to build, and carried both road and rail traffic. They tested its weight by driving eight locomotives on to the roof, which would carry the rail traffic. We're great at building stuff that goes out of date quickly, and such was the train part of the crossing, falling out of use just twelve years after opening.

Glass and Pyrex
Sunderland's long history of glass production started in the seventh century when Benedict Biscop employed glaziers from Rome and France to make stained-glass windows for the Monkwearmouth monastery. The first glasshouses opened in Deptford, Sunderland, in the

Grinding domestic glassware at Wear Glassworks, 1922. (Sunderland Museum and Winter Gardens)

Inspecting and packing Pyrex labware at Wear Glassworks, 1922. (Sunderland Museum and Winter Gardens)

James A. Jobling poster for Pyrex. (Sunderland Museum and Winter Gardens)

1690s making items like windows and bottles for export, and by the 1800s Sunderland had seven bottleworks and three glassworks. Production continued to grow and as technology developed, it became quick and cost effective to produce it in larger quantities.

Popular Sunderland glass company J.A. Jobling & Co. Ltd saw a downturn in business and so Ernest Jobling Purser (the nephew of James A. Jobling) bought the rights to an oven-proof glass technique from America called Pyrex. Despite being produced in the US for at least ten years, in 1922 it breathed new life into Sunderland's glass industry. Pyrex was marketed directly to housewives and quickly became an integral part of every kitchen. Joblings used the ration shortages of the Second World War to their advantage, and pushed the idea of saving on waste by making casseroles using leftovers, in Pyrex dishes. As popularity soared, Jopling's took out a license to sell worldwide and soon everyone who had a Pyrex dish had a little piece of Sunderland in their home.

Car Manufacturing and Nissan

Mention car manufacturing in the UK and Japanese company Nissan will be one of the first words that springs to mind. Mention it in Sunderland and it'll be first, every time. As one of Sunderland's biggest employers, Nissan arrived at a time of great industrial loss, just when the town needed it most.

Nissan had been bringing cars to the UK from Japan for a while before the Sunderland plant was built, since the late 1960s. As the popularity of their cars grew, homegrown car

Sunderland airport, 1984. (Nissan)

companies like British Leyland were starting to decline. Nissan started to look at building a plant in the UK, and initially a few sites were considered, before they settled on the former site of RAF Usworth and, later, Sunderland Airport.

In September 1986, she whose name is mud in the mining villages of County Durham and Northumberland, Margaret Thatcher, opened the new Nissan plant – the first in Europe – along with Nissan president Yutaka Katayama. Production had actually started a couple of months before, and in July the first new car rolled off the production line: a Nissan Bluebird. Bluebirds, in their many incarnations over the years, were one of the most recognised sedans internationally. Known for their reliability and long life, they were popular for almost five decades, though they stopped producing them in Sunderland in 1990.

Nissan had a small staff initially, starting out with just 500 people and building 5,000 cars in the first year. When production of the Bluebird ended, they started to build the Primera and just two years later in 1992 the Micra, meaning Nissan were producing two models at their Sunderland plant. By this time production was up to half a million vehicles in total. The following year, Nissan were awarded the Queen's Award for Export Achievement as well as the RSA Environmental Award. A year later it was given a Gold Award by the Royal Society for the Prevention of Accidents and a year after that, it hit the one million mark for cars produced.

It was then that things took a turn for Nissan. Sales of the Primera were slow, causing Nissan to join forces with Renault. An economic downturn followed and Nissan laid off

Breaking ground at Nissan. (Nissan)

Phase one of building complete. (Nissan)

around 800 employees. It soon bounced back though, and the production of the Qashqai and Juke were to thank for that in large part.

Technology was, of course, improving all the while, and soon Nissan were hitting their 5 million production milestone. Where the production of a Bluebird would take twenty-two hours, a Qashqai could now be built in eight and a half. Nissan received another Queen's Award for Export in 2010, which was also the year they started to build a plant to make batteries for the Leaf Electric car, planned from 2012. In 2013, Nissan started to produce the 100 per cent electric Leaf and the new Nissan Note started production. The plant was also substantially extended to include more space for the body shop and production lines.

The plant was visited by royalty in 2015 when Prince Charles arrived to see the production lines and speak to some of the students who were part of Nissan's new Skills Foundation – a programme designed to get kids excited about STEM (science, technology, engineering and maths) careers.

The British motor industry as a whole has seen a 50 per cent fall in investment, and coupled with the fall in sale of diesel cars and economic uncertainty that the country faces as it looks at leaving the EU, it's hit Nissan hard.

While it's business as usual as much as possible – Nissan vehicles were the first cars over shiny new bridge Northern Spire in 2018 – its future is far from guaranteed, and with some 40,000 jobs linked to the Sunderland plant, both directly and through feeder factories, all we can do is wait and hope that the Japanese-Sunderland relationship isn't over yet.

Opening of the South Dock by Mark Thompson. (Sunderland Museum and Winter Gardens)

Henry Hay Wake and Roker Pier

In 1868, at the young age of twenty-five, Sunderland-born Henry Hay Wake became the Chief Engineer of the River Wear Commissioners. He succeeded his mentor Thomas Meik after Meik's retirement, and continued his work in reshaping Sunderland docks.

The original North Dock had been designed by Isambard Kingdom Brunell, but by the time it opened in 1837 it was already inadequate for the growing need to transport coal. Ships were getting bigger too, and the dock just couldn't cope. Sunderland Dock Company was formed in 1846 and a South Dock was built that could hold 260 vessels, opening in 1850 and extended a few years later. As time progressed, the piers were also becoming unfit for purpose, and so Wake began working on plans to create a new harbour and piers, which were approved.

Dignitaries assembled on Roker Pier, 1895. (Sunderland Museum and Winter Gardens)

Laying a 45-ton block on Roker Pier, 1895. (Sunderland Museum and Winter Gardens)

The Opening of Roker Pier and Lighthouse by the Earl of Durham, 1903. (Sunderland Museum and Winter Gardens)

Construction of the new North Pier (now Roker Pier) began in 1885 with the lighthouse opening in 1903. Under the pier was a tunnel that carried gas pipes and also served the very useful function of allowing the lighthouse keeper to get to the lighthouse in bad weather, when waves would have made walking along the top incredibly dangerous. Henry Hay Wake had plaques with his children's initials installed in the tunnel underneath Roker Pier. It's also rumoured that behind one of the stones, that of Enid H. Wake, is a gold sovereign.

As well as changing the look and functionality of the port and harbour, Wake designed the Wear Dredger (known as 'Wear' – a 130 feet long vessel that arrived on the Wear after trials in 1881) and the heavy-weight crane nicknamed 'Goliath', which was used to build Roker Pier, transporting concrete blocks for the base that weighed up to 56 tons.

Wake retired in 1907 and took up a position as consulting engineer to the Wear Commissioners, which he did until his death in 1911 at the age of sixty-seven.

An extensive restoration of Roker Pier and Lighthouse began in 2012 and was recently completed. As well as sympathetically restoring the inside of the lighthouse, the tunnels were also made safe, and for the first time it is now possible to take a guided tour of the tunnel, before climbing to the very top of the lighthouse for one of the best views in Sunderland.

Aerial view of the Port of Sunderland, 2017. (Sunderland Museum and Winter Gardens)

Roker Pier and Lighthouse, 2018.

Vaux Breweries

At one time, Vaux Breweries was the heart of Sunderland. Beloved for their great beers and community involvement, Vaux, even today, are remembered with affection. Vaux was so much more than just beer production, the threads of the company run through Sunderland's history and their effects linger.

Vaux drays being loaded for delivery. (Sunderland Museum and Winter Gardens)

Vaux Breweries, 1920s. (Sunderland Museum and Winter Gardens)

Cuthbert Vaux was first involved with brewing in 1806 but Vaux only formed their own brewery in 1837, starting on the corner of Matlock Street and Cumberland Street in Sunderland. They moved to Union Street in 1844 and then again in 1875, this time between Castle Street and Gillbridge Avenue.

Vaux started to brew a beer called Maxim Ale in 1901 to celebrate the return of the Maxim gun detachment led by Ernest Vaux in the Boer War. The beer proved to be a little too effective, causing landlords to complain that their customers were falling asleep due to its potency. If a customer was asleep they couldn't buy more beer, and so the strength of Maxim was reduced. Now known as Double Maxim and still brewed today, it's one of the country's oldest surviving beers.

Ernest Vaux was very much involved with his community, and near the site of the brewery was the Garrison Field (where Keel Square is now), which housed the 7th DLI, who were formed in 1908. The first Scout troop listed in the Imperial Records was started here by Vaux and was visited by Robert Baden-Powell in February 1908, over a year after his Brownsea Island camp where Scouting is considered to have officially started.

Vaux horses and dray, 1949. (Sunderland Museum and Winter Gardens)

By now the Nicholson family were running the brewery, Frank Nicholson joining in 1897 as manager and secretary. His brothers-in-law didn't want him to have any shares in the brewery, but they did promote him to managing director in 1919 as rumour has it that they were a little too fond of the product to manage the business effectively. In 1927 the company merged with North Eastern Breweries and became known as Vaux and Associated Breweries.

As Vaux was growing, a little pub called The Brewery Tap (which has also been known as The Neptune, The Number Nine, and The Minerva) was prospering too, and had been jogging along quite nicely since the mid-1800s. It spent a brief time as a smallpox hospital in 1869 before returning to a pub again in 1872. Perfectly placed to be a flagship pub for Vaux (it was right in the middle of town, next to the brewery), there was only one small issue: it belonged to their rivals, Whitbread. This was a bit embarrassing for Vaux, so they started negotiations to bring it into their portfolio. Of course, Whitbread were fully aware of the importance of The Brewery Tap and dug their heels in until Vaux were forced to exchange it for one of their best earning Tyneside pubs, The Clousden Hill Inn at Forest Hall.

Sadly, the brewery was not to last, and due to in-house disagreements with its board it closed its doors in 1999. While many will only know the word Vaux associated with beer and perhaps sponsorship of Sunderland's football club, there's so much more: starting the first Scout troop in the country, naming a beer after a machine gun, and a turf war with a rival brewery are only some of the reasons that Vaux was never 'just a brewery' to Sunderland, but something that had personality and heart, so that it was and still is part of the city's soul.

The Wearmouth Bridge

The Wearmouth Bridge is arguably the pride of Sunderland. Instantly recognisable to locals (annoyingly sometimes confused with the Tyne Bridge by non-locals), it's the last bridge before the River Wear opens up into the North Sea.

What many don't realise is that our beloved green 'through arch' is actually the third incarnation of the bridge. In 1796, the first bridge (known then as Iron Bridge) opened and was the second largest cast-iron bridge in the world as well as the biggest single-span iron bridge in the world. Designed by Thomas Paine, it arched high over the river – 100 feet from the bottom of the bridge to the low water mark – to allow sailing ships to pass. Until now, anyone wanting to get to the other side of the river would either have had a long trip to the closest bridge in Chester-le-Street, or would have needed to hop on the

Etching of Iron Bridge. (Sunderland Museum and Winter Gardens)

The construction of Wearmouth Bridge, almost complete, 10 February 1929. (Sunderland Museum and Winter Gardens)

ferry. Once the bridge was complete, it was very popular, so much so that for a short while there was a toll for pedestrians to cross, as well as other traffic.

By the early 1800s, parts were starting to bulge and loosen from exposure to the weather, and so after being patched up in dribs and drabs for a while, it was stripped back, had all new ironwork added, was widened, and had its distinctive 'hump' straightened out. Our 'new' bridge opened in 1859. In those days, it doesn't seem like we were building things to last, as in the early 1900s the bridge was once again showing signs of deterioration, particularly from the increasing popularity of the motor car.

Doing major works on something constantly in use is always difficult, and taking away the function of a bridge in particular can have a huge effect on a town. In 1927, when construction on the new (and current) bridge started, engineers built around the existing bridge to allow the road to stay open and in use.

The Wearmouth Bridge, as we know it today, opened two years later in 1929 with the future king (George VI, then the Duke of York) in attendance. The Wearmouth Bridge is still a Sunderland icon, and hasn't been overshadowed by the Queen Alexandra Bridge, the Hylton Bridge or by its new, slightly more glamourous, sibling Northern Spire.

Northern Spire, which opened in 2018, is the newest addition to the Wear's crossings.

Conclusion

One person's secret is another's boasting right, and very few of us are able to resist the temptation to 'well actually' when we get excited by facts, figures, myths and legends. This is how stories are continued, are passed down the generations, and it's something to be celebrated.

When I started researching this book, my first step was initiating conversations, sitting down with people who, like me, had long been immersed in Sunderland's past and who were able, with passion and enthusiasm, to point me in directions that I might not otherwise have looked. I think of this book as a longer version of those conversations – something I hope will make you dig a little deeper, find a little more, or even just pass along your favourite tales.

It can be a hard balance to write something interesting and compelling, without sensationalising, or using something – a tragedy like the Victoria Hall stampede, for example – as entertainment. I hope I've walked this tightrope well enough, and do strongly believe that you can't rewrite, gloss over or whitewash history. In order to learn from it, we must become comfortable hearing about and discussing the darker sides of our past.

If you've read this far then Sunderland has revealed some of its secrets to you. Does it have more secrets to share? Undoubtedly.

Roker beach.

Penshaw Monument.

Bibliography and Further Reading

Books:

Anderson, Albert, *The Victoria Hall Disaster* (Black Cat Publishing)

Gardiner, Marie, *Sunderland Industrial Giant: Recollections of Working Life* (The History Press, 2017)

Johnson, Michael, *The Sunderland Cottage: A History of Wearside's 'Little Palaces'* (Amberley Publishing, 2015)

Norman, Bill, *Luftwaffe Losses Over Northumberland and Durham 1939–1945* (Pen & Sword Books, 2003)

Robinson, Alistair, *Sunderland Empire: A Centenary History* (The History Press, 2007)

Spencer, Alfred, *Life of Harry Watts; Sixty Years Sailor & Diver* (HardPress Publishing, 2012)

Websites:

BBC History: www.bbc.co.uk/history

Durham at War: www.durhamatwar.org.uk

Grace's Guide: www.gracesguide.co.uk

Historic England: www.historicengland.org.uk

North of England Civic Trust: www.nect.org.uk

Sunderland Association Football Club: www.safc.com

Smithsonian Institution: www.si.edu

Sunderland Echo: www.sunderlandecho.com

The Sunderland Site (Searle Canada): www.searlecanada.org

The Wartime Memories Project: www.wartimememoriesproject.com

Acknowledgements

Anyone can write a book if they put their minds to it, but it takes a number of people to really make it work. To that end, I'd like to extend my thanks to a few of them.

Matthew Storey and Frank Nicholson, who very generously took time out of their busy schedules to share their vast knowledge and passion of Sunderland with me. I'm immensely grateful to you both.

Thanks also to John Stelling, Stuart Miller and Dave Walmsley for being at the other end of an email to keep me right when I'm wading into their specialist fields.

Special thanks must go once again to the wonderful keepers of our history, at the various archives: Jo Cunningham and the team at Sunderland Museum and Winter Gardens, Julie Boad and staff at the Sunderland Local Studies Library, and Julian Harrop at Beamish Living Museum of the North. The importance of these archives can't be overstated and they are generally underfunded and understaffed, so all the more to be appreciated. Thanks, too, to Louise Wandless at the Stadium of Light.

As a photographer as well as a writer, it has been my privilege to be given permission to photograph some of our wonderful old buildings. My grateful thanks to Kelly and Guru Gobind Singh Sikh Temple, to Claire Pickersgill, Adam Rowbotham and Mikey Smith at the Sunderland Empire Theatre, and to Grindon Hall School.

Finally, thanks to Lisa, who keeps me sane when I'm up to the eyes in research and, as always, to Mark, who has put up with at least eight months of complaining.